Redefining Happiness

How to Be Happy on Your Own Terms

Kelli von Heydekampf

Redefining Happiness: How to Be Happy on Your Own Terms

By Kelli von Heydekampf

First printing: 2021

ISBN-13: 978-1-7374590-0-2

Kelli von Heydekampf

West Metro Hypnosis

6545 Flying Cloud Drive

Eden Prairie, MN 55344

952-222-3975

kelli@kellivon.com

www.kellivon.com / www.westmetrohypnosis.com

Kelli von Heydekampf is available for your next speaking engagement on a variety of topics.

To Mathias,

For defining happiness with me.

"Life is amazing. And then it is awful. And then it's amazing again. And in between the amazing and the awful it's ordinary and mundane and routine. Breathe in the amazing, hold on through the awful, and relax and exhale during the ordinary. That's just living heartbreaking, soul-healing, amazing, awful, ordinary life. And it's breathtakingly beautiful [...]"

~ LR Knost

Table of Contents

CHAPTER 1

Is This It?

What do you do when everything you've been taught about being happy doesn't work? What happens when you realize that you've checked all the boxes of the proverbial happiness equation, and yet that happiness you've been promised continues to elude you? How do you reconcile the illusion of the "perfect" out there when it doesn't match the inside? What do you do when you realize you aren't happy?

Standing in my beautiful home, in my well-maintained and safe neighborhood, I came to the jolting conclusion that this was my reality. Without fully understanding all of the above questions being asked of me, I had to admit that I was not happy, despite the perfection of everything in my external world. And it wasn't that I was unhappy either. The feeling I was experiencing was like an absence of something, a letdown; I felt like I kept striving to get to happiness, but its arrival remained elusive. I felt like I had not yet arrived even though I had checked off all the boxes that I was taught were part of the happiness equation. Its presence—elusive, non-existent. (Or so I thought.) Standing alone in my house that day, these thoughts left me feeling ashamed, embarrassed, and guilty.

It wasn't that I wasn't capable of moments of joy; I also wasn't experiencing depression either. It was a moment of absolute clarity to realize I had done everything according to *The List*, and yet the feeling I thought its achievement was supposed to evoke alluded me. I felt robbed, wondering when and how happiness was supposed to arrive. I was thirty-two years old. We had moved to the United States the year prior as my husband had been promoted to a new position that required him to be at headquarters in Minnesota. Prior to that, we had been living in Germany, where I had spent the last thirteen years. My life had not been without challenges and hardships; we all have the traumas that life deals us with, but I know I was living an enviable life. Why wasn't I able to fully enjoy it?

My three girls were at those magical ages where pretending, curiosity, and imagination are the main playmates. My husband had a great job that he enjoyed and provided a life beyond everyday comforts. Our marriage was solid. Except for the occasional cold, everyone was healthy. We had nice cars, a beautiful home, and took exotic vacations. I had the choice to stay at home and raise our daughters, and I threw myself wholeheartedly into that role. I had done everything I was taught to do. I had achieved all the things I was taught to achieve. I had attained all the goals I was taught were important. The checklist was complete, finished, done.

When I mention *The List*, perhaps you are familiar with it as well. *The List* contains all those things that we have been taught and shown from an early age that will produce happiness. My prescribed list included but was not limited to:

- being excellent in school so I could get into college;
- going to college;
- getting a "good" job;
- finding the person I would marry;
- having kids;
- accumulating nice things; and
- going on great vacations.

Just writing out this list, I realize how benign the process was for me to accept these things as the path to happiness. I never questioned their validity because they are valid aspects of a fulfilled life. Back then, they were simply points on the journey that I assumed were the "have to's" the "supposed to's," and the "shoulds" that created the happiness formula. There is a whole lot of space in between those points that I didn't understand was the space to find happiness. I wish I had understood that "the destination is the journey" because the things on my list and the people involved contributed in magnificent ways to my contentment with my life. I wish I had known how to appreciate and enjoy them more.

I am fortunate to have been able to achieve my list early in my life. I am fully aware that this is not the case for most people. All the more reason I felt ashamed, guilty, and undeserving of all of my blessings. At that moment, standing in the entryway of the home I loved, I realized that I had to change something. It couldn't possibly be true that I was to continue feeling a sense of lack, a sense of not enough, and a sense of being stressed in the midst of all of the abundance I had! Something was off. If I couldn't be happy, who could be?

The promise I had bought into didn't deliver. So, what did I do? I made a choice to investigate. I didn't know how or with whom or how long, but thankfully, I listened to a voice whispering that **this** wasn't it. I wasn't doomed to a life of striving, pursuing, and attaining without reward. I just had to unlearn much of what I (and everyone around me) had been taught. To find it, I first had to forget happiness. I had to forget everything that I had been taught about it and about pursuing it.

~ ~ ~

It's been nearly 20 years since that lightning bolt moment of clarity. Looking back, it's hard to know everything that has taken place within that time, but the journey that has brought me to this moment has allowed me to be more at peace, more present, and more accepting of everything that is, including more fully loving of myself. So, what is the solution? If the list is only one part of the equation and not the full solution, what is the answer to being happy? And why does it allude so many of us despite the abundance in which many of us live?

The pursuit of happiness does not guarantee happiness. I get what our Founding Fathers were trying to go for with this statement, and it sounds noble. This pursuit is as American as apple pie, baseball, and the Fourth of July. We learn about it from a young age and believe it to be a worthy goal to pursue. We believe in the promise, the inspiration, and even its achievability. So why are so many of us still waiting for happiness to manifest? Well, words matter. Not only do words matter but the context of words matters. In the time and the space in which those words were first written, it made sense to foster and protect the idea that we should enjoy the freedoms that allow us to go about our lives in a way that ensures the freedoms to determine our own courses and be responsible for our own development. In the face of the many persecutions, restrictions, and restraints that our founding countrymen were dealing with, the idea to pursue our own happiness was a radical one. The intention was good and, for the time, absolutely appropriate.

The practice of pursuing happiness in the twenty-first century has many of us questioning its validity. Achieving happiness has become a glorified to-do list, always keeping us in *attainment mode*: *If I do A, B, C, and D, then I'll be happy.* Or, *If I have X, Y, and Z, then I'll be happy.* This formula has been spoon-fed to us culturally for decades as most of us continue to wonder, *When will it finally happen? When can I finally get off the hamster wheel of life and just be happy?* The problem with this is that most of us don't even know *how* to define happiness. We have that as our main goal in life, and yet when asked to define it, we can't; it remains nebulous, vague, and indefinite.

Don't get me wrong, the pursuit of happiness has helped us in many ways. Many great people have achieved great things in light of this pursuit. It has made many of us productive, responsible, engaging citizens. And that is where the difference is. In our pursuit, waiting to attain, reach and achieve, we frequently overlook all that is around us that provides for contentment *right now*. We have so fallen for and often unknowingly accepted the idea of doing the ABCs to get the XYZs that we no longer participate in the present. Culturally, this way of life is not only very accepted but also expected. The formula—*go to school, work hard, go to college, work hard, get a job, work hard, have a family, work hard until you retire*—has been going on for decades. So, what do you do when you've checked off all the boxes, fulfilled the to-do list, accomplished everything you were taught to do, and happiness still eludes you? What then? What else is there to pursue? If happiness was the goal and it remains out of reach after attaining everything, then what?

The solution, of course, is simple, effective, and very straightforward, as most effective solutions are. The solution is choice. I know, I know, it's so cliché, right? But remember, I said it was simple. I didn't say it was easy. The simplest things are not always the easiest to do. I had a *lot* to unlearn before I could make the choice to be happy. Much of that unlearning had to do with just the definition of happiness. What is happy? How do you define it? What does it mean? We walk around saying that we just want to be happy, and yet very few of us take the time to define it. Most of us stay on that hamster wheel, trying our best to check off the items on the list that we never stop to ask ourselves, what is it that I want for me, my family, and my life? We shove it off into the future, always thinking that once A, B, C, and D are accomplished, *then* we'll be happy. How much of your life are you willing to give away to someone else's terms, conditions, and definitions?

One definition of "happy" (according to Cambridge Dictionary) is "feeling, showing, or causing pleasure or satisfaction," which is a straightforward, acceptable definition. The two belief barriers that keep us from our well-being and that are so embedded into our Western Culture are:

1. the idea that pleasure and satisfaction come from outside things, circumstances, and environments; and

2. the belief that if we are feeling anything *but* happy, we must be doing something wrong.

We see these beliefs constantly perpetuated through advertising. We've built an entire industry making sure we feel inadequate unless we have the latest flavor of the day, and when these pleasurable feelings wear off, the next new shining object, drug, or thing is just a purchase away. These two coupled ideas keep so many of us right there on that hamster wheel of pursuing, trying, and achieving that it usually takes a big-bang type moment of awareness to finally decide to do something different and push the barriers of the conventional.

This book offers a guide for you to experience a higher degree of freedom in defining your own happiness, based on the experience I had making the choice to become a participant in my own life. As an active participant, I had to start making choices. And define things. And let other things go. And learn, explore, discover, and play at a different level. *And* to stop *trying* to be happy and let go of all the loaded messages around that concept. Giving up that need was a vital step in my journey. My hope is that you will give yourself permission to become curious about your own life. Perhaps the most important thing this book offers is the questions that it poses so that you too can become a more engaged participant in your own journey, more clearly define what a happy life looks like to you, and cultivate the willingness to create it in ways that feel right and authentic to you and the people most important to you.

Whether I am supporting my kids, spouse, or clients, (or myself), I have found that one of the most important things I can do is ask questions. We are each our own experts, and when we trust that we can discover our own best solutions, we lead our most authentic lives. High-quality questions deliver high-quality answers.

Are you ready to discover what your answers are?

As you read through this book, see how my journey can begin to lay a foundation for exploring and finding your own new and best path. Use my insights to deepen your inner awareness. Use my questions to gain and foster your inner wisdom. And most importantly, use this time for yourself to give happiness an updated definition. Be brave enough to define it for yourself on your terms. Make that choice for yourself now.

Questions to contemplate:

1. What has your definition of happy been up to this point?

2. How does suspending your current idea of happiness lead you to important self-reflection and discovery?

3. What are five things that are most important to you as it pertains to being happy?

CHAPTER 2

Our Basic Humanness

Once I had identified the "problem" of my inability to be happy, the first choice I had to make was whether or not I was willing to do something about it. This is where free will comes in. I didn't have to move forward. No one was pushing me to change, so why bother? My family didn't know that I was unhappy and if you had asked me, I would not have said I was unhappy. But there was definitely a longing, a feeling of something missing.

Written into every seed is the information necessary for it to become whatever its code says it will become—an acorn grows into an oak tree; a sunflower seed grows into the sunflower; a caterpillar grows into a butterfly. This information is hardwired into the very smallest particle of what that entity is to become. So, what does that mean for you and me, members of the human race? I believe it means that we come hardwired as well. If an acorn already has all the information it needs to become a mighty oak tree, why would we have anything less? Factored into its ability to become the best oak tree it can become are environmental circumstances. Does this acorn take root in favorable soil? Does it get adequate sunlight, water, and other nutrients? Does it get too much of something? All of these things play a role in its growth, but the information to *thrive* is already there. We've all seen those trees that grow in odd directions because of environmental factors— either leaning in at precarious angles or shooting out of riverbanks. The tree does its best with what it has to thrive, sometimes even defying the very environment itself. How easy is it for you to accept that you are already coded to thrive? And what does thriving even mean?

If you've ever taken a psychology course, you learned about Maslow's Hierarchy of Needs. This is the outline of needs that must be met for us humans to advance to higher levels of fulfillment. The first two foundations meet the requirements that encompass surviving or having our basic needs met. These include adequate food, shelter, rest, and the feeling of being safe. Once these basic needs are met, we move into the areas where thriving can begin to take root: our human need for belonging and meaningful relationships; our desire to feel needed and purposeful; and lastly, our wish to unfold our highest potential and manifest our unique creativity. (When you look at this, you can see how our advertising industry directs us to stay at the level of survival--the level in which outside factors remain the focus of our well-being.)

This hierarchy of needs encapsulates the information that is already coded into us. Our very beingness comes complete with these needs, desires, and potential wired in us. This implies that learning, growing, and discovering all that we are is part of the course, the very essence of being human. We can't help it. It doesn't mean all of us always reach our highest and greatest potential, but it does mean that we are creative beings with a persistent desire to know "what else?"

It is the very question of "What else?" that launches us into our next level of discovery. And it is precisely the question I was asking myself as I became aware that those outside factors weren't fulfilling the promise that I had bought into for so long. "What else?" can also be asked as "is this it?" which is where I was at. Looking back, I realize this internal desire to know a deeper truth of my own potential allowed me to suspend my current beliefs and reliability on an illusion system for creating happiness. Our creative nature moves us forward into the asking, investigating, and exploring that is required to unlock potential. And in all of that, nowhere is it written that this takes place without struggle, challenges, and unknowing. The journey really is the destination because as soon as we reach one destination, it's only a matter of time before we ask ourselves, *What else?*

Starting from "is this it?" allowed me to get curious about what else life had in store for me. Trust me, I do realize that my "this is it" was pretty darn good. So good that many people would have been satisfied with it. But that is the beauty of happiness, creativity, and self-discovery. There is no limit. There is no completion. There is no point where we arrive and say there is nothing left—unless we decide it. That is a choice as well. We get free will every step of the way. And the discovery that I have made is that when we go on that journey of "what else," we are supported and guided in ways that aren't even imaginable. It isn't always an easy choice to make because we are required to step in and be willing to play, participate, and take actions sometimes in ways that we aren't sure we can do.

At this point, we could argue that it isn't the pursuit of happiness that should be forgotten but actually only updated. If pursuing, discovering, and pushing to the next level is part of our humanness, then maybe the more important questions to ask are *what* you are pursuing and to *what end* are you pursuing it? Therein lies the road to true happiness. It is in the redefining of the path that you discover the pleasure and satisfaction we all seek. The coveted destination becomes the appreciation of the journey.

Questions to Contemplate:

1. What have you currently been pursuing, and to what end? According to whose terms?

2. What else is waiting for you to discover about who you are and why you have your particular set of gifts, talents, and skills?

3. Can you begin to believe that as you make choices for yourself, that resources become available in ways that perhaps you haven't even considered? What keeps you from stepping into this belief more fully?

CHAPTER 3

Striving for Happiness

"**W**ell, I just want to be happy." This is my most recent client—mid-thirties, business owner, great family, and doing well financially. He has no real reason to be *UNhappy*. This is my most favorite kind of client because this person KNOWS they SHOULD be happy and yet wonders what they are doing wrong. The system is rigged.

The United States spends more on advertising than any other country in the world (China being second). From an early age, we are bombarded with pictures, images, and dialogues that promise us the formula *product = happiness*. Building on our human instincts to avoid pain and move towards pleasure, we are guided to an endless assortment of have-to-haves to ensure that we belong, that we are validated, and are on the right track to success. And it doesn't matter what age. These factors are in play for young kids starting at the checkout counter of any grocery store and grow in importance as we move through the teenage years and adulthood. (When I was a teenager, to be "in," you had to have Lagoon shorts, Vans, and Izod shirts. Do you remember having to have that *thing* otherwise, you would simply die?) These ornaments are dangled in front of us, holding so much promise and power. And because they seem to temporarily fill the *avoid pain, move toward pleasure* gap, we rely on the process to fill us up again and again.

In my forgetting everything I had been taught about happiness, I came to a point where I realized I had done nothing wrong. Everything I was feeling: emptiness, disempowered, unfilled, was exactly what I was set up to be feeling based on the system. Lynne Twist, author of *The Soul of Money - Transforming Your Relationship with Money and Life*, defines this system as the "sea of cultural conditioning in which we all swim." She describes the bombardment of information to consumers as a "tsunami of messaging" to keep us in the cycle of perpetual desire, wanting, and feeling "less than." She identifies three toxic lies that make up this sea of cultural conditioning that are necessary to keep the pattern going. (Keep in mind the context is speaking about affluent, first-world countries.) The first toxic lie she speaks about is the belief of scarcity—that there simply isn't enough to go around. If we believe this, then we believe we have to make sure we get what we can get, when we can get it. We have to fight for what is ours. And if someone else gets something, it leaves less for me and mine. Someone will be left out, and I don't want it to be me. (You may recognize this as an accepted marketing tool; create scarcity to get people to buy now.) Scarcity is not limited to just money. It spreads like a disease through so many other systems as well: not enough time, not enough energy, not enough people, not enough love, not enough resources, and on and on.

Toxic lie number two is "more is better"—more space, more cars, more jewelry, more vacations, more food than we can eat, more clothes than we can wear, more everything. The other side of this idea is that we have to keep getting more before we can share with others. The concept of more relies upon *more* and *enough* never being defined. In terms of giving and sharing, we repeatedly think, *When I have XYZ amount, then I can share.* Except when that amount is reached, we still don't feel like we have enough to share. The final toxic lie is, "This is just the way things are." This conditioning and these beliefs seem bigger than us, so there isn't anything we can do about it. We often believe that we're just another consumer in the cog, so we as individuals, can't affect any sort of meaningful change. This thought leaves us feeling like the only option we have is staying on the hamster wheel and keeping up with the Joneses.

Our culture of consuming needs us to keep believing that we are not enough unless we fulfill the circumstantial criteria of success, and it is one of the most significant contributors to keeping us from experiencing deeper degrees of joy, satisfaction, and contentment. This is why questioning becomes so important (more on that later). If we constantly rely on a culturally accepted definition of "happiness" and rely on a system that only focuses on outward environmental factors, we will never discover our own truths about what it means to be joyful, fulfilled, and have balance in our lives. This brings me back to Steve, my client, saying, "I just want to be happy."

I asked Steve what that meant. He looked at me, confused like the thought of defining the concept had never crossed his mind. (I knew that feeling too). Surprised as well that there may be some internal work involved that he hadn't considered.

So, I asked him, "How will you know when you are happy?"

And he replied, "I don't know. I guess I'll be excited. And I'll smile more."

Me: "Do you have to be excited all the time for you to be happy?"

Steve: "Yes, I think ... isn't that how it's supposed to be?"

Me: "I think you get to choose how happy feels to you."

Steve looks relieved.

Me: "If smiling is an indicator of you being happy, what needs to happen in order for you to smile?"

Steve: "Nothing, I suppose. I could just smile right now if I wanted to."

Me: "What is keeping you from smiling right now?"

Steve says nothing. He just smiles.

You may be thinking that this is way too simple of a process. The most effective processes to move us forward are very simple—they aren't always easy to implement but they are often simple. What is important to recognize in this exchange is the role of questions. If we never take the time to define what it is we want to experience, how will we know when we are experiencing it? I think that so many of us are walking around with a diluted version of this word "happiness" that none of us know what it means to us on a *personal* level. Without questions, we stay in the cyclone of outside situations and constantly rely on circumstances to determine our emotional states. There must be a better way.

The Teeter-Totter of Human Emotions

Remember being a kid and playing on a teeter-totter? You could have a whole group of kids and divide them up to see how many kids were needed to go up, go down or maintain perfect balance. You could even walk along it yourself, like a balance beam, and see if you could get it to balance on your own, for yourself. This metaphor helps demonstrate how expanding the definition of happiness can broaden the scope of feeling to be more inclusive of more experiences. Bringing us to the awareness that we are actually doing a lot of things right already—we just weren't giving ourselves credit for any of it. (When you only focus on what you think is broken, you don't realize how much is working.)

If you look at the whole spectrum of emotion possible within the human experience, it ranges anywhere from despair all the way to bliss (thus the teeter-totter metaphor). When you look at all the different options, it seems silly to box ourselves into one all-encompassing emotion. The pallet is so much richer than that. This is why defining it is so important. People ultimately want to experience longer periods of positive, affirming emotional states and can move into those states more effectively when they have options. These options allow us to have a choice so we can be the people we want to be. (Without options, you have no choice.) We know that life will not guarantee us a smooth ride without bumps, roadblocks, and uphill climbs, so why do we judge ourselves so harshly about our emotions? Emotional states are temporary. And they are all appropriate and normal. So, if emotional states are temporary and they are all appropriate, can we begin to accept that we have more power to influence them than we may have realized? And when we realize this power, how do we begin to use it to influence our emotional states and our relationship with them?

My client, Steve, believed the ultimate goal was a constant state of happiness. Like me, that is what he had been taught and what was causing a disconnect. He had made the assumption, "If I am anything but happy, I haven't achieved success. Therefore, I have to keep working to fix it, to achieve it, to get there." Steve also connected the feeling of excitement to happiness. When we dug deeper into that, he admitted that being excited all the time actually sounded kind of exhausting. When we began expanding and identifying his pallet of options, he discovered that there were quite a few go-to's he could choose to make him feel successful in creating a more positive foundational emotional state and experience it more often. He also began to realize that he wasn't as unhappy as he thought himself to be. He was starting to realize that it was within his power to define his own contentment. This concept correlates perfectly with *emotional granularity*, which is the ability to specifically identify what a person is experiencing and understand the array of emotional options that are available at any given time. Without this, people tend to globalize their emotions between pleasure and displeasure without any awareness of the different distinctions.

When we begin to unpack this large umbrella of "happiness," a couple of things tend to be realized. One of them is acknowledging that we have many more episodes of positive emotional states that we tend to easily dismiss and disregard because they aren't accompanied by the level of excitement we often connect with happiness. (Think of all the advertisements and social media posts you have seen in your lifetime that depict a *particular kind* of happiness.) Also, our minds tend to focus on what needs to be fixed, improved, or changed, and so many of us have become experts in conditioning ourselves to believe that we aren't enough, haven't yet done enough, and don't have enough to be able to fully arrive at that coveted place of constant bliss. The collective conditioning of our culture reinforces this idea as well, so it seems perfectly normal to think, *Once I do this, have this thing or become this, I will be happy.*

Another realization is a deeper level of acceptance of the individual ways and the differing degrees that happiness can be experienced. This can be seen by looking at the spectrum of emotions and validating that peace, calm, and balance can definitely be experienced as forms of happiness. When we can accept the whole teeter-totter of emotions, we begin to see how many options we have. And isn't exactly the entirety of the spectrum that creates our rich experience of life? How boring would it be if this teeter-totter didn't exist? How bland would our lives be?

There is a spot on that teeter-totter that most of us don't even accept as an option when it comes to an emotional choice. (Probably because we've never really been taught to see it as an offering.) It is right there in the middle, that perfect place of balance, where you haven't tipped into the heavier *negative* emotions and aren't yet ascending into the lighter *positive* emotions—a place you could say is emotionless, empty, or void. I like to refer to this spot as beingness. It's a place where we can be without expectation, need, or requirement to feel anything; a state of being present and open without needing to judge; a state where you can feel what it's like to be you in your body without the need to qualify or quantify any of your experience. It's you realizing that nothing else is needed. It's a place of suspension where you can take a moment to renew before moving out and moving on.

Getting to a place where we accept *all* emotion as a normal part of the human experience is important in our development. So many of us spend so much time judging ourselves in positive and negative ways, depending on the emotions that are being experienced. In my work with clients, I no longer label emotions as positive or negative just because of all the judgment wrapped up in those descriptions. It is very appropriate at times to feel deep sadness, just like it is to feel anger or disappointment. I have moved *away* from positive and negative *to* contracting emotions and expansive emotions, mainly focusing on how they show up as a physical response in the body—as in contracting within the body. This gives people something to work with, a starting point where they can identify what they are experiencing and ask themselves if it benefits them. They can then determine how long they want to stay there, working from the understanding that they can begin to effectively move into a more beneficial state (further up on the scale). Change the body's physical state from tight contraction into open expansiveness, and the emotional state will begin to follow.

Let me emphasize this again. Change the physical state of the body, and the emotional/mental state will begin to change as well. If the body is the vessel in which emotions are contained, then there must be congruence between the substance being held and the container holding the substance. You don't hold boiling hot water in a plastic container, right? When we hold on to contracting emotions, the body will reflect that. Every client I ask to describe the physical sensations of their contracting emotions, use words like tight, resistance, tension, hot, fast, buzzing, looping, solid, heavy, weighing down, stuck, etc. When I guide them through a series of exercises to induce the body into relaxation and then ask them to describe what the matching emotion feels like, they respond with peace, calm, resilience, quiet, light, slow, wavy, etc. It can be so much easier to change the physical response than it can to change the emotional one.

The first step in releasing physical tension and constriction in the body is to breath. (Simple, right?) Slow and deepen your breath and the body will release tension. Dogs do this all the time and I often tell clients to use their dogs as a model to periodically do the "dog sigh", letting go of all tension and tightness, a moment of complete release. We can do this even in the midst of emotional turmoil. Knowing this information allows people a choice and a tool to take themselves out of an emotionally contractive pattern at will. It allows space to put aside judgments surrounding whatever emotional state is being experienced and move to understanding and accepting that contractive emotional states are okay and normal. It is empowering to know that I can choose how long I remain in that state.

To help clients accept the normalcy of all emotions, I point out the world of duality in which we all live.

Hot/cold, straight/narrow, lack/abundance, etc. We can think of duality as being the two sides of the same coin. When we begin to realize and practice looking at the other side of whatever coin we are using, we discover an option there, perhaps that we have not contemplated. I offer my ten top emotional states here, which can help you recognize that if you can feel the heavier one, you also come with the ability to feel the lighter side as well. The capacity to feel and be both is there in us. But we have to make a choice; we have to choose to flip over the coin. With the list below, I challenge you to take some time and feel into all of these and see how they feel specifically to you in your body. What is the physicality of each of these? How are they the same? How are they different? What does this awareness offer you as far as moving out of unbeneficial states?

1	Anxiety/Anxiousness	Resilience
2	Worry	Trust
3	Despair	Hope
4	Resentfulness	Forgiving
5	Shame	Pride
6	Guilt	Innocence
7	Overwhelm	Empowered
8	Confusion	Clarity
9	Doubt	Confident
10	Frustration	Calm

Personally, this realization of defining my emotional states and giving myself permission to expand my options was very powerful. It allowed me to let go of the idea that there was a particular way I thought I was supposed to feel in order to receive the "happiness stamp of approval." That's what I had been waiting for. And because I was in a constant state of waiting for this thing to happen, for this state to arrive, I couldn't even see what was right before my eyes—that it was me who needed to change what I was seeing.

Questions to contemplate:

1. What limitations have you put on your definition of happiness?

2. Where can you start giving yourself credit for things you're doing well or *right?*

3. What does "beingness" feel like to you? How do you think this state can benefit you?

CHAPTER 4

The Power of Questions

In today's world, when we have a question, we go to the internet. "Hey, Google. Who was the seventeenth President?" "Hey, Siri. How do I make baklava?" The internet never doesn't come up with an answer. It always provides some sort of response even if it doesn't answer our question. Your mind is similar. You ask it a question, and it will provide some sort of response, even if it doesn't give you the answer you want.

Big changes, transformation usually begin with one moment, a moment of clarity where suddenly we can see things we hadn't seen before—moments of awareness. Change never happens without awareness. It's the precursor to change. My big moment of awareness was standing in my house, pinpointing with absolute clarity that I was not happy. That moment of awareness that you experience, however, isn't enough. It isn't sufficient to know what you don't want or to know what isn't working. There must be a next step, a plan of action, a path from dark to light. But we don't know what we don't know, so how do we know what to do?

Hindsight is 20/20, and while you are going through "stuff," it's hard to know if what you are doing is *right* or helpful. Looking back over the years, I know that the decisions I ended up making were beneficial for me, but life isn't a choose-your-own-adventure book where you can go back and compare the outcomes and endings. (I always thought that would be so cool!) I began to recognize some of the patterns that I found myself perpetuating. In that moment of clarity, where I was able to admit things were not working for me, I didn't necessarily have answers, but I did have questions. This is the brilliance of those kinds of moments. The mind will provide answers to our questions because it does not like open loops. However, the quality of our answers will always rely on the quality of our questions. I had been asking very low-quality questions.

In my opinion, some of the most overrated, low-quality questions begin with *why*." Why do I feel this way? Why am I stuck? Why can't I get over this?

Why can't I feel differently? It wasn't until studying hypnosis did I begin to see how limiting these kinds of questions are. Knowing that the subconscious mind has a record of all experiences, feelings, and memories to answers those why questions, the subconscious mind scans all of its files within milliseconds and then delivers the answers. The answers always come in the form of the cause as we state the effect. *Why* questions are cause/effect questions, and they are based on *past* information. Information that most likely was impressed upon us by both skilled and unskilled people from our past. We are not taught that at some point, we get to *question* that information beyond asking only why. Below are some typical why questions and answers:

- Why am I afraid of public speaking?
  - Because I was made fun of in school about how I talk.
- Why can't I commit to healthy relationships?
  - Because I only saw abusive ones and anything else feels unfamiliar.
- Why do I always comfort myself with food?
  - Because it has made me feel better in the past.

I am not completely discounting asking and seeking answers to our why questions. It can be very important and useful to know and understand information about our past. The key factor for me is, does this information and understanding move you forward in beneficial ways, or does it just keep you looping around in circles, coming back to the same places you've been, feeling like you're going nowhere? If the answers don't help you find a path forward, then there's missing information that still needs to be discovered.

The high-quality questions that can provide new information usually come in the form of hows and whats. I consider these to be high-quality questions because they require the creative mind to forge new paths, consider new ideas, and map out new directions. For example, it wasn't enough for me to ask why I was unhappy. At the end of the day, none of the reasons mattered because they weren't relevant. I wasn't fighting for my existence, didn't have a devastating childhood, and didn't want or need for anything, so asking *why* wasn't ever going to give me an answer that would sufficiently move me out of that pattern. What was I going to do about it? What was I willing to change? How would I go about finding new answers? What unbeneficial patterns could I identify where I was stuck and what was I willing to do to change those patterns? How would happiness feel if it finally arrived? These are the kinds of questions that delivered new and different results. They weren't asked all at once, but it was through the unfolding of a questioning process that allowed for creative answers, solutions, and resources to be identified and explored.

The moment we realize that we can actually begin to question things is the moment we realize our power. To give ourselves permission to let go of the Belief Systems (to let go of the BS) that no longer work for us and to begin to decidedly create what we want is something that doesn't just happen. You have to be willing to participate. You have to be willing to ask the kinds of questions that put not only the responsibility on you to create change but place the power fully in your hands to move forward. That can be very scary. It can be scary because it means we have to start seeing ourselves more fully, more honestly, and be willing to trust more completely.

As I continued to seek the sources for my lack of happiness, I began to discover and identify the patterns that I had fallen into that weren't beneficial. At the time, these patterns didn't seem unbeneficial because they felt so familiar. (Familiar is not always beneficial and what is beneficial is not always familiar.) The more I learned and understood how patterns and programs are formed in the first place, the easier it was for me to step outside of those patterns, knowing that there was nothing *wrong* with me. I was able to disconnect from self-blame.

Let's talk about how patterns are formed. We discussed cultural conditioning earlier. This conditioning begins from the moment we are born (experts say even starting in-vitro), and the sphere of influence expands as time goes on and we grow. The sphere is usually limited to close family at the beginning and then expands to include extended family, friends, neighbors, community, church, school, etc. This conditioning can be seen as learning what is important for us to be successful in our particular environment and it happens all at a subconscious level. We arrive in this world without awareness of consciousness. Our awareness grows over time, but the first approximately seven years of life is spent taking in information subconsciously. This is good because the subconscious mind is so much more efficient at processing information. Arriving in your particular human experience, you have to figure out how to be as successful as you can be in the environment you find yourself in and with the people who surround you. Because there is so much information that the mind must filter to decipher what information is most important for you to be successful, the subconscious mind pays particular attention to certain pieces of information while disregarding the rest. Because the subconscious mind doesn't judge what is going on as good or bad, right or wrong, it needs parameters to determine what is important. What is important can be broken down into five different categories, and this is what the subconscious mind pays attention to. (They are in no particular order of importance.)

Categories of Important Imformation

The first category is people of authority. The mind differentiates between those people only playing support roles and the people closest to us and the experts we seek who are the main characters playing "People of Authority". These are typically our original caregivers, whether those are our parents, grandparents, foster parents, siblings etc. They are the people around us "showing us the ropes" and they have an indelible impact on what we come to believe about our world. (This is the reason why, when I travel with my older sister, I still ask for her approval on what I am wearing.) Later, these people include teachers, clergy, work supervisors, experts like doctors, police officers etc. Because of our inexperience and lack of knowledge, we rely on this group of authority to show and tell us how the world works—in whatever world we find ourselves. In our youthful innocence, we aren't aware of our ability to question these people and what they say, do, or think, so we simply accept the truths they share with us whether they are good, bad, right, wrong, and everything in between.

Emotionally charged experiences is the second category and are a way for the mind to sift out important information. It does not matter whether the experiences are emotional in a positive, nurturing way or a negative, damaging experience; the subconscious mind identifies both as beneficial pieces of information. Emotion adds weight to an experience, raising it to the level of flagging it as something that needs to be paid attention to so that in the future, the subconscious mind can support you in moving towards what is beneficial or protecting you from what is harmful or dangerous.

Category three is about repetition. Practice makes permanent. The subconscious mind pays attention to repetition. Things that happen again and again or things that are practiced over and over will be noted as important. The subconscious mind will program anything it can in order to be more efficient. Forget going for perfect because practice, practice, practice makes programs! It really is a good thing that the mind can shortcut stuff because it makes learning easier. This is a beneficial tool for so many things. Think about if you had to relearn driving a car every time you went somewhere. Remember, the subconscious never judges and always identifies a positive intention behind a behavior dependent of the information being provided. As the subconscious becomes more efficient in its programs, it can begins to associate things that logically make no sense and generalizes information to cover bases that may or may not be important; it is one of the reasons why people with fears, phobias, and anxiety (just to name a few) typically report that these issues get worse over time. The subconscious mind is simply doing what it does. An example of this is when a fear of public speaking all of sudden leaves someone unable to make a phone call—the subconscious mind has generalized information and associated more specific things into the realm of what is to be feared, all in the name of efficiency. (Which means there is nothing WRONG with you!)

The influence of peer groups can never be underestimated, which is why this is another category of information the subconscious mind relies upon. Humans have a need and desire to belong to a group, a tribe, a circle of equals. It is a source from which we know our identity, importance, and place in the world. As we get older, our peers and what they think of us carry remarkable influence on how we perceive ourselves. Perhaps you remember back to those teenage years and recall how the prospect of being accepted (or not being accepted) by peers sometimes became all-consuming. Peer groups continue to play a role in our identity even well into adulthood. They provide so much of the specific way we see ourselves--through the different labels we attach to whatever identifier we pursue—religious affiliation, political affiliation, professional affiliation, and on and on. As you mature, you have the freedom to determine how much power you will give these peer groups to determine your path and your level of contentment. Are you just following the pack so you have a place to belong? Does the pack align with who you truly want to be?

Lastly, the subconscious mind can learn and respond very quickly, and we know this as the power of suggestion which is the last category we look at as to how the subconscious filters information. New information can be introduced to the mind in a way so it doesn't first critique it. It simply responds to the suggestion and readily accepts it. I refer to the example of a police car parked on the shoulder of a highway. We see it and respond by slowing down, checking our speed, or both, even if we aren't speeding. The police car at that moment is the suggestion and it elicits an immediate response. Advertisers know how powerful suggestions can be, which is why advertising is a multi-billion-dollar industry. It is also why hypnosis works.

The process of information filtering and program production is going on in the mind all the time, but it is at its highest capacity during the stages of infant, toddler, and early childhood. You may be familiar with the phrase, "Give me a child until he is seven and I will show you the man," which illustrates perfectly the process of information being formed and impressed upon us because the mind must quickly figure out how to be successful and manage the world in which we find ourselves. The information is accepted as truth without critiquing it.

All of these things together make up what I refer to as the collective conditioning all of us are exposed to, without judgment. It becomes the filter through which we see our tiny little world. It is the information that is *passively* impressed upon us. Understanding how the mind formulates its programs and patterns is truly enlightening. It allows us to step out of the scene for a moment, look at it and understand that we are never doing it wrong. Our choices and behaviors reflect what we have come to believe about our world. Therefore, we do not need to be fixed. We only need to grow and expand our beliefs, our truths and our worldviews. When we take a moment to investigate, we discover that our behaviors are usually congruent with the program, which is congruent with the beliefs that we have collected over a lifetime through our relationships and our experiences from the different ways described above. Everything is working perfectly according to that formula. We don't have to beat ourselves up for not doing it differently. This is the blanket answer to "Why do I do the things I do?" The outcome matches the input.

But we are not mere robots. Just like you can update a computer by downloading new information, you can do the same thing with new thoughts and actions using the information provided above about how the subconscious mind learns, moving from passive acceptance to active questioning and deliberate choices that lead to change. You can step out of the collective conditioning. As I mentioned earlier, patterns and programs are not always providing us with what we want, but as long as the subconscious mind sees them as beneficial, they stay in place.

Perhaps you are hoping to find solutions to various issues you have been dealing with for a long time. Many people's belief systems have been formed based on the information above. Perhaps you are struggling with anxiety, attention deficit hyperactivity disorder (ADHD), self-doubt, or lack of self-worth. Maybe you aren't sleeping and have been struggling for a long time. We can easily break down these examples and match them to their respective categories:

An anxiety diagnosis is usually delivered via a person of authority—a medical doctor—and is typically validated through other professionals.[1] Suppose you had experiences of not fitting in as a child because you didn't look like other children. In that case, these emotionally charged incidents are an important contributing factor. Maybe these were not one-time events but repeated in different environments and situations often enough for the mind to flag these experiences as important

---

[1] I do not contest the validity of the diagnosis; I simply point out the power of statements made by professionals. Too often, diagnoses are presented as dead-ends instead of building bridges that offer hope to be able to be productive, responsible and capable DESPITE the diagnosis.

(repetition). These incidents can lead to feelings of not belonging, which further leads to self-doubt and self-worth questions (lack of peer group). Being told of one's inability to focus (power of suggestion) helps create a belief that one would always struggle in school and professional life.

One of the most damaging patterns I realized was affecting my ability to be happy, and one that I began questioning was the program of my perceived source of self-value, worth, and importance. I believed my worth existed equally to how busy, stressed, and burdened I was. Maybe you too recognize this "busyness syndrome". Collective conditioning led me to believe that to feel, claim and know my worth, I had to have a full schedule; a full to-do list all the time; say yes to everything that was asked of me even if it meant my response and fulfillment of it might be from a complete passive-aggressive state; not have time for myself; let others around me know how busy, stressed and burdened I was; and on and on. I didn't feel like I could enjoy the great life I had because that would be selfish, and being selfish is bad. I had it so good that there was an underlying belief that I was supposed to feel guilty about my good fortune. It was my job to control *everything* otherwise, I wasn't a good wife and mother. If I wasn't overwhelmed, I wasn't contributing, and I wasn't of value. It was a lot to unpack and unlearn.

Everyone wants to be of value; it is a human need and desire hard-wired into us. Those passively accepted subconscious beliefs of mine, I thought, meant there was no choice but to be stressed and overwhelmed to be worthy. This means I was the one creating the situations where I felt overwhelmed and stressed in order to validate myself. It wasn't an outside experience; my inner beliefs were the very things creating my worldly experience. What an astounding understanding! Left to its own devices, my mind kept creating familiar patterns to validate those beliefs, perpetuating the same outcomes.

Again, I was fortunate enough to be in a life situation where I had resources of time, money, and energy to explore these things, making growth and self-development more accessible. No matter your particular environmental circumstances, the realization that you can only see and experience what your filter allows is a valuable lesson. We can't see what we don't see. Taking inventory of fundamental beliefs can be beneficial in identifying the ways that our filters are limiting us. We all have beliefs around how safe we feel in the world, what it means to be in relationships, our self-worth, purpose and attitude, beliefs around money, and what we are able to achieve. All of our perceived limitations are self-imposed, which implies that liberation is self-induced as well.

Consider this analogy about your ability to formulate high-quality questions: your mind is the internet, and your intellect is like YouTube. The totality of your mind has a record of all experiences (whether you remember them or not). Based on those experiences and the beliefs created from those experiences, your mind creates channels just like YouTube. You can google anything, and you will always be provided an answer. Your intellect and imagination can do this as well. Ask it anything, and it will provide an answer of some sort. The more you dial in what you put in the search bar, the more specific the answer. Your mind creates content, all kinds of it, at its own will. It can reason its way into doing *anything* or reason its way out of doing something. To claim your true power, you must recognize that the intellect is at its best when *you* are the master; otherwise, you are simply following different YouTube channels based on suggestions. You can change the channel, turn it down, turn it off, or create new content, but know that you are ultimately in charge of your thinking.

The acronym S.T.O.P. can help remind you of that power:

Space **T**ime **O**f **P**ossibility

Use this space and this moment to simply S.T.O.P. and think of a new possibility and then do something different without getting caught up in the overanalyzing of it. One small action that allows you to be successful is the first step in creating new patterns and behaviors, and you have all the internal resources necessary to begin to make positive changes, sometimes you simply need to stop and pause.

Questions to contemplate:

1. What are your beliefs around the following: self-worth, purpose, money, relationships, and attitude?

2. What are the sources of your passively accepted beliefs, and how have they been limiting you?

3. What actions or thoughts can you change that will take you in a new, more beneficial direction?

CHAPTER 5

Change the Input to
Change the Outcome

This book is being written during 2020/2021 among a global pandemic, major civil unrest, and a major divided political climate in the U.S. Norms, beliefs, and tolerated behaviors are being questioned, if not downright shattered. Now more than ever, we need people who are willing to define their destinies.

For my personal journey of *defining my destiny*, finding happiness, this appeared to be a daunting task, like it was some sort of event that was supposed to happen with a definite start and an even more defined finish that included a triumphant celebration that I had "made it." What is even more interesting is that I never thought about what was to happen *after* I made it! It is a question that I choose to no longer entertain because the answer seems to be either impossible to imagine or unacceptable even to contemplate. When I think of that now, it creates a sort of disappointment, like the journey would be over, and now I just have to settle.

If you are at a point like I was where you are ready to experience a different way of seeing things, a new perspective, and a deeper understanding of your life, I offer you a question that you can begin to ask yourself. The question is one that not only helped me in my moment of awareness that I wanted something different, but it continues to help me as I grow and explore all that life offers-- even the challenges.

That question is: ***What else?***

- *What else* can I learn?
- *What else* am I called to do?
- *What else* is there besides the accumulation of "stuff"?
- *What else* is there besides the hamster wheel?
- *What else* connects me to the people around me besides blood, marriage, friendship, community?
- *What else* is mine to do?

- *What else* am I here to feel?
- *What else* is there beyond survival, scraping by, only making ends meet?
- *What else* is there beyond differences, division, and separateness?

Take a moment to *feel* or experience this question. *What else?* Even if you don't immediately get an answer, can you feel how it opens up to possibility? How it beckons curiosity? How it calls to your imagination to want to, at the very least, begin to explore? I am fully aware that we can use the same question in the negative. What else can go wrong? What else will fail me? What else will I miss? etc. This is the power of choice we have. Will you ask the questions that perpetuate "stuckness," or will you use your wildly creative mind to explore and investigate?

One of the things that I started to notice about asking these kinds of questions was (and is) how quickly resources appeared when starting to explore answers. Over the years, those resources have varied from parenting classes to books, mentors, spirituality guides and coaches. These resources allowed me to explore a deeper need that I had only begun to recognize as a personal, spiritual need. I now know that instead of the finality of the event that I had sought, I realized that this is what life is about—the consistency of the journey that appears in the form of a new day, a new moment, a new opportunity. I was so busy rushing up the hill to get to the finish line (believing this was what was expected of me) that I didn't even realize how much of the landscape around me I was missing. Looking back, I realize how this robbed me of being present with my children and husband and how many moments I took for granted in the hurriedness of striving and just getting stuff done so it could be "accomplished."

I also realize how my experiences of "stuckness" offered opportunities to push through old patterns by presenting just the right experiences that challenged the very thinking that restricted me and kept me in the conformity of the outer circumstances and expectations. Patterns can only keep you stuck as long as we are willing to participate in them. They are the very learning environment provided for us to grow and go to the next level. Without them, how would we ever know what growth we are capable of? A baby learns to walk only by first falling down.

Paying attention to what is in the realm of my control and influence allows me to direct my time, energy, and resources in a way that produces feelings of empowerment, resilience, and competency. More importantly, it allows me to feel like I am doing something to add to the collective consciousness in meaningful ways. When we take steps to break out of unbeneficial thinking and patterns, we pave the way for others to do so as well. The things that are always within our control and are definitely part of the input are our words, thoughts, feelings, and actions. The importance of being someone who is willing to take responsibility for their own thoughts, words, actions and feelings cannot be underestimated!

Our circumstances seem at times so overwhelming that we can wonder how any possible improvements and changes can be realized. The adage: "peace begins with me" is so very true. Growth begins with me. Positivity begins with me. A good attitude begins with me. Health begins with me. Empowerment begins with me. We must be willing to be the change we wish to see, no matter how small or insignificant that change may seem. This is different for every single person. What is important to me may not be important to you in terms of how we show up and where we spend our energy. It's good that we don't all want to pursue the same things. But if I can be responsible for me and the little corner of my world and you have the space to do the same, can we see how this might begin to add positive changes over time?

We will never see the kinds of change and growth we desire in our lives, our communities, and our world unless we are willing to be the conduit for growth, expansion, and willingness to show up and be accountable. That means it is essential to take the time, even if it is a short moment, to establish that which you wish to experience. If you wish to be calmer, then you must practice calm. You must first be willing to acknowledge it in yourself, despite what outside circumstances appear to be dictating. You must practice it. You must be willing to see it in yourself without quantifying it or qualifying it, or disregarding it. Even if it only lasts a moment, acknowledge it, validate your ability to experience it, and begin to nurture it. This is what it means to change the input. You change the input, and you change the outcome.

Coming back from a really wonderful vacation and renewing time, I remember walking in through the door of our home and immediately feeling the weight of *everything* I felt needed to get done—right now. Simply walking through the door triggered my mental "to-do" list, which caused my old belief of self-worth being tied to productivity to flare up. After all, I had just spent the last few weeks being anything but productive, and so I had to make up for "lost time," said my mind. This all happened in nanoseconds. The onslaught of overwhelm that I felt was enormous yet also utterly ridiculous. I had just arrived home from vacation, so of course, there were things I needed to do but was I going to sacrifice all the great feelings I came home with for laundry and grocery shopping?

Reacting to overwhelm (of my creation) had been my mode of operation for many years, but I was so surprised to see it flare up so easily and quickly. I thought I had done so much to address it. The gift here, though, was in the moment of awareness. I recognized my pattern and knew that I could choose how long I wished to stay and participate in it. If I wanted a different experience, I simply had to do something different. I decided to listen to a hypnosis recording I had about having enough time—the very thing I felt I didn't have. I decided to change the input. I took twenty minutes to listen and remind myself that I had all the time I needed to get done what was important and that everything would get done in the right and perfect time and order. Taking responsibility for giving myself what I needed to reframe my experience allowed me to show up in a more congruent way with who I wanted to be and what I wanted to model. The "doing something different" could have been any number of things: a few moments of breathing, a quick walk around the block, a re-do of walking into the house again with a different mindset, a call to a friend or mentor. There isn't a set prescription. Just do *something* different, use this space and time of possibility (S.T.O.P.) and make a different choice, change the input to change the outcome.

The world of recovery has given us many valuable tools to address everyday challenges in our lives, whether or not they are tied to addiction. In order to change the input, I have found great value in tools that I learned from recovery programs. Both of them are connected to personal responsibility and control of things we have control.

The first is using the acronym H.A.L.T. which stands for **H**unger, **A**ngry, **L**onely, **T**ired. To create the foundation for any recovery, we must be willing to care for these personal needs. I often think that I am in recovery from limited thinking, so it is just as important for me to pay attention to these as it is for someone who is in recovery from substance addiction. Ensuring I meet my needs of satisfying hunger, working through anger, taking steps to address my loneliness (need for connection), and ensuring I get adequate sleep are methods to control the input in meaningful ways. It doesn't promise automatic smooth sailing, but it ensures that the basics are covered. It also gives me a starting point to address things when I feel out of control. Is it because I am hungry, angry, lonely, or tired? If I can't meet those needs right now, how does my awareness of those needs allow me to be gentle with myself until I can, without giving up responsibility to meet them? If it isn't one of those, at least I have addressed my basic needs and can continue to investigate.

This brings me to the second tool which is declarative statements starting with: "I need, I want, I feel ..." Declarative statements declare facts that provide the other person with information. I walked around for years believing that other people (primarily close family members) should just know how I feel or what I want and need. I assumed that they should know me well enough to read my mind. Guess what? They didn't, and they don't. Just like I don't know what it is they need, want, or feel. I frequently fall into the trap of thinking I know what they need, feel, and want. Mother knows best, right? I have improved in this area, but there is room to grow. When we can state clearly, how we feel, what we need, and what we want, it doesn't mean that the other person can deliver. It does mean that we take responsibility for offering information that will allow others to know how they can show up for us. Often, we are happily surprised at the response we get. Both tools are ways for you to ensure that you take responsibility for things that are within your control.

The last tool I offer is an equation that I have on the wall of my office that I refer to as the *Success Equation* and supports the idea of "change the input to change the output." If you look at the power of the mind and how we use it, it illustrates perfectly what is going on all the time. Whether we use this power consciously in meaningful ways is up to us. Perhaps it is a way to see the law of attraction as well. The equation is:

$$A^2 + S/T \times F = O$$

Let's break this down, starting with the end first.

$$A^2 + S/T \times F = \mathbf{O}$$

The **O** stands for the ***outcome***. You will always have an outcome. You always have had an outcome. Your life will unfold and continue to happen. Do you want to participate in your outcome, or will it simply continue to happen *to* you?

In order to participate more fully in the creation of your outcome, you need the rest of the equation.

$$A^2 + S/T \times F = O$$

The first **A** in A^2 stands for ***awareness***. You need a moment of awareness, either of where you are, where you want to go, or both. Remember, awareness gives you clarity; clarity unconfuses the mind, which frees up internal resources to congruently be directed in a new direction. Confusion (overanalyzing) keeps you stuck. This brings us to the second **A** for ***action***. Awareness alone will not move you forward. Moving forward is an action, and you must *do* something to move forward. That action may be in the form of tweaking how you are "being," and yes, *being* is an action. Habits and patterns are created by taking the same actions repeatedly. Even passive actions like thinking. Do something that will move you in the direction of your desired outcome. It doesn't have to be big, and it doesn't have to be all at once—small, subtly different actions taken consistently over time yield significant results.

$$A^2 + \mathbf{S/T} \times F = O$$

Now let's discuss **S/T**. We live in a world of physical matter, ***space*** and ***time***. This means that matter (outcome) requires us to be in a process. Things don't materialize all at once. We have to move through space and time to arrive at our outcome. So much frustration is experienced by wanting our outcome *right now* or believing it should arrive in a certain way or on a certain timeline. We forget that our timeline is not always the only timeline or the best timeline. As we continue to take appropriate action consistently, we can remind ourselves, *This is what it looks like as it all comes together*. It is also important to be aware space and time happen *only* right now. Our intellect understands that we have done things in the past. It also understands how we can plan to do something in the future. Our subconscious mind (SCM) (which is our *presence—* our ability to be un-self-conscious) understands only *right now*. Right now is the only moment we have to think, feel a feeling, or take an action. Right now, on the spectrum of space and time is your moment of empowerment or your moment of disempowerment. Which will you choose?

$$A^2 + S/T \times \mathbf{F} = 0$$

The final part of the equation is about our free will and our ability to choose. ***Focus***. As creative beings, we can choose our focus. Awareness helps us realize where our focus is; actions can help us redirect our focus. We can focus on our outcome and *trust* that this is happening as we take the steps required; we can focus on internal resources that will support us in taking consistent actions; we can focus on our successes; we can focus on what our perceived failures have taught us so we can learn from them; we can always focus on limitation, lack and all the ways life is against us. We get to choose. It isn't always easy to choose your focus, and sometimes we need to be gentle with ourselves and take a break from doing, doing, doing. But your focus will determine the lens through which you see your opportunities, your possibilities, and your ability to create the life *you* desire.

It is important to note that focus does not imply ongoing conscious attention to one thing. Focus is not willpower. Anything that requires us to pay attention to it 100% will ultimately exhaust us. My clients who want to give up smoking frequently believe that they do not have enough willpower to quit. When I explain to them that willpower is an unsustainable resource and does not have anything to do with their success at becoming a non-smoker, they are invariably relieved. We switch their focus from quitting smoking to remaining smoke-free, which directs all of their choices in a completely different direction and not having to pay attention to quitting, which the mind perceives as deprivation. This frees up internal resources that can be used to choose different options that support the outcome of remaining smoke-free. Simply put, focus determines your direction.

Questions to contemplate:

1. What else is there for you to experience in this life?

2. In what ways has your input limited your outcome?

3. How can you use the success formula to establish a new way of looking at your life?

CHAPTER 6

A Purpose Driven Life

I had always envied people who knew what they were going to be when they grew up. That sense of knowing so deeply that you never question your purpose must be a feeling of definitive certainty that helps put structure around life decisions. Those of us who have not known our purpose or who have changed our purpose, question where we are on our journey simply because we have not experienced that sense of deep knowing.

Many of us have heard the saying, "The destination is the journey," but what does that mean on a day-to-day, moment-by-moment level? For those of us waiting for our purpose to materialize, what if we chose what we want it to be for the moment until something better presents itself? For some, their purpose is their profession and their passion. For many others, their professions or jobs are merely a means to pay the bills and put food on the table. In both of these scenarios, we can establish a higher purpose that envelopes whichever category we find ourselves.

If you feel you are without purpose, what if you made one up? In Japanese, the purpose of life is *ikigai* and can be translated to "a life worth living." In a BBC article, "Ikigai: A Japanese concept to improve work and life," the author, Yukari Mitsuhashi, writes, "Essentially, ikigai is the reason why you get up in the morning." This means different things to different people, but the result comes from the belief "that the sum of small joys in everyday life results in more fulfilling life as a whole." For *ikigai* to be at play, this means that those small joys show up as actions (small or large) in service to others. Service to others is described in the article as "purpose in action," which, to me, is not about the action per se but the attitude in which we perform the action. This shift in attitude, a re-focusing of how we see the same action, can lead to a higher degree of personal contentment. If you are in a job that you do not like right now, what would happen if you took a moment to identify all the different ways you bring value and how your actions affect the whole? Could you perhaps begin to feel better about where you are right now?

At one point in my life, I was a life-skills presenter at different high schools. I would go in and deliver various workshops for classes that taught specific skills. One of my favorite workshops was on interviewing for jobs. Explaining the interviewing process to high schoolers as an opportunity to present one's value and worth to a potential company was a new concept to most of them. One of the activities I would have them do is identify the tasks of their current jobs and figure out the value that it brought. For instance, someone who was working at McDonald's said they were responsible for taking out the trash and cleaning. To this student, the job was a basic skills job and therefore, in their mind, wasn't worthy of feeling good about it. When we broke it down and talked about what would happen if they didn't do their job well— eating areas would be disgusting, trash would pile up, people wouldn't want to eat there, the department of health could potentially fine the establishment, etc.—they began to see the importance of the job and how it held a lot of value. In reformulating the task to a skill, they were able to see that what they were doing was maintaining a clean and inviting environment that upheld the standards of the health department. Did this ultimately mean that they were doing anything different? No, but the potential to shift their attitude to feel good about the work they were doing was now at least established. Whether they chose to show up differently was now up to them. We can find purpose or *ikigai* in anything we do if we are willing to look for it. That shift in attitude might be the very thing needed to move us to our next best self.

In the past, I often felt that finding my life's purpose just felt too big and overwhelming. I have decided that it is okay for it to be defined in very small increments of time—what is mine to do right now? This purpose also includes the challenges, the days that don't feel so good, the moments where I find myself questioning my value, worth, and what this all means. Coming to realize that there must be an acceptance of *all of it* was one of the most beneficial moments of clarity for me. (It is something that I find myself needing to RE-mind myself of often.) The acceptance of challenging moments is by no means an acceptance of permanence that this is how it's going to be forever. It is merely a moment of knowing that everything is exactly as it is right now. Accepting what *is* allows me to claim the power that lies within my choice of action I take based on my awareness at the time, which means, in moments of uncertainty, my purpose is always right there: to show up in the best way I can, with what I have at the moment. If I can consistently show up with the purpose of being a positive force in this world and take responsibility for the moments I am not, then it doesn't matter if I am folding laundry, preparing a meal, walking the dog, or helping a client; I will actively be contributing to my *ikigai*.

Remember, too, the beautiful thing about your purpose is that you get to make it up. Take a moment to take that in. *You get to make it up.* If you don't know what it is, or if you are unsure, make something up. Maybe for today, it's to bring your neighbor groceries. Or to color with your toddler. Or to cook a meal for your family. Maybe it's to deal with loss or cry or grieve or be angry at the injustices of the world, which propels you to an action of a higher calling. We get to make it up. Will you define your purpose (as I once did) through the lens of outward expectation, or will you take a moment to reflect and choose to design it yourself?

All creation begins with a thought. If you want to build a chair, you must first think about the kind of chair you want to make. How big will it be? What will it be made of? What purpose will it serve? You may have moments where you think about what kind of chair you don't want, but ultimately, you must put your focus, energy, and time into creating the image of what you do want. It may change with time as the building process unfolds but you must start with a blueprint that lays out a plan so you can begin. As we hold on to that picture or idea, we find that our minds begin to identify resources that help us fulfill the end goal. What blueprint are you creating in your mind about you and your purpose? What picture are you holding onto of yourself as you show up every day? Do you remember those foundational properties of love, creativity, and power? Do you remember your capacity to learn and grow? Do you see yourself as capable, worthy, and deserving? How will you change unless you see yourself differently? When you feel stuck, do you hold on to your inability to free yourself or entertain the idea of moving forward? These are big questions that can feel overwhelming. You don't build a chair all in one step. There is a process, a start, and a finish. Bring it down to a level that feels manageable. Identify one thing that you want to believe about yourself or about your purpose in life and begin to create a more beneficial picture that you can hold in your mind. And begin to believe you can grow.

Personally, I like the idea of growing instead of changing. Changing, to me, implies that there is something wrong that needs to be fixed--like a light bulb that is burnt out. However, growth implies that where I am is exactly where I need to be right now, *and* there is another level for me to grow into. Where I am now is a necessary part of the process; otherwise, how will I learn what I need to know to get me to the next level? Too often, we think in absolutes. That we only have an either/or option. What if you started more often to think in both/and terms? By this, I mean that we can be scared and still do the thing that terrifies us. Eleanor Roosevelt encouraged this in her famous quote, "You gain strength, courage, and confidence by every experience in which you really stop to look fear in the face." You can *not* want to do something and still do it. You can feel doubt and still learn how to trust. You can feel unloved, unworthy, undeserving and still begin to believe that there is a different story for yourself. It is the growing process where you move out of one state and into another, and that is a fabulous purpose to have in itself!

Another way I began to look at the purpose of life was from Bruce Lipton. He is one of my favorite resources I continue to use to remind myself of this journey and possibility. He is also the author of *The*

Biology of Belief and one of the early scientists in epigenetics. Dr. Lipton has talked about his own questioning of "what does all of this mean and what is my purpose?" He tells the story of how he was contemplating these questions, and in a moment of undeniable clarity, he heard a voice. The voice answered, "Because Spirit wants to know what chocolate tastes like." At first, this may seem like a silly answer, but it is rather profound upon further exploration. If we can accept that there is a life force within each of us that creates a unique expression of life (call it Spirit, the soul, divine energy— however you define it) and your physical body is the vehicle that this life force uses to navigate the earthly world, then doesn't it make sense that this energy relies on the combination of your senses, personality, physical traits, and abilities to experience all that life offers? It relies on *you* for *it* to be able to taste what chocolate tastes like, to feel what it's like to hike a mountain, to kiss for the first time. Being a unique expression of life means that this deeper part of ourselves is a constant in its knowing our foundational properties of love, creativity, and power. It is our human side that forgets. We are free will beings with the capacity and the ability to choose; choose our words, actions, feelings, thoughts, and focus. Part of our purpose in the journey is simply to *remember* who we are beyond the limitations of our identities.

"Keep it simple" is a mantra in the recovery world, and it is a wonderful reminder to all of us. Our purpose is right in front of us. Whatever you do, can you do it with more presence? Can you do it in a way that allows you to be a model for others? Is part of your purpose to give up that which no longer serves you: whether it be guilt, anger, the need to be right, the need to control? Can you expand your own capacity for joy, curiosity, and exploration? Can you allow yourself to trust in having a purpose even if it isn't defined and clear? And what if your purpose is simply to get out of your head and into this moment to its fullest? Purpose is a quantum leap, not a step-by-step path of instruction.

I end this chapter with the Word of the Day from the *Daily Word Magazine*, Thursday, November 19, 2020, where "purpose" is beautifully described:

Purpose

I live a life of purpose.

What am I doing with my life, my time here on earth? What is my purpose? I begin my search for answers by realizing I am not here to be defined by my interests, my gender, my physical appearance, or my education. I am so much more than any of those aspects of me.

I have something special and distinct to offer. Made in the image of God, I am here to know and live from my spiritual identity. As I express gratitude, acceptance, and kindness to others, I am helping to fulfill my life's purpose as an expression of the Divine.

The more fully I act in accordance with my purpose, the more fulfilled I feel. I am grateful to live with passion and clarity.

http://www.dailyword.com/

Questions to contemplate:

1. What would it feel like to lead into a greater purpose, even if it unfolds moment by moment?

2. If your job/profession is not your purpose, what can you do to nurture your purpose outside of work and allow it to flourish?

3. What brings you joy? What purpose can you find in that? What if you transferred those same feelings to things that aren't fulfilling or don't feel purposeful?

CHAPTER 7

Rules of the Mind

A helpful tool that I learned along the way is the Eight Rules of the Mind. This list was not attributed to anyone when I first learned it, and I have not been able to find a source for it. It is a powerful outline of how to delineate the usage of the different departments of the mind and, when used appropriately, create congruency between the conscious and subconscious to work on our behalf. Let's dive into these *rules* and see how we can apply them to our benefit.

1. Imagination is more powerful than knowledge when dealing with your mind or the mind of another.

"Imagination is more important than knowledge."

"Logic will get you from A to B. Imagination will take you anywhere."

Both of these quotes from Albert Einstein demonstrate his own belief in the power of imagination and explain the first rule's importance. If you understand that everything is first created in mind, then this rule makes perfect sense. Before anything becomes *real,"* we first have to imagine what that thing is. Whether it is a tangible, physical thing or an intangible, emotional thing, our imagination is playing the main role in our perception of reality, whether we realize it or not. The ability to wield our imagination to focus on what we choose is one of the most powerful practices we can execute in our day-to-day experience. The mind does not differentiate between that which is intensely and emotionally imagined and that which is real. (This is the reason why when we watch a horror movie, our body responds as if danger were lurking.) Knowing that we have a natural pull towards the negative, we must be willing to imagine positive, beneficial outcomes, even when we feel it difficult to get there. Without imagination, thoughts stay in an intellectual realm and have difficulty ever leaving the logical part of our mind. Once you combine them with the power of imagination, you create an experience. Your creative mind can begin to create pathways of making the imagined real.

2. Opposing ideas cannot be held at the same time.

Right now, make a fist with your right hand and clench it tightly. While you are clenching your hand into a fist, relax the same hand. You cannot do it. Opposing ideas cannot be held at the same time. You have to choose whether you will relax the hand or clench it. Both cannot be done at the same time. This is the dilemma that we are often posed to deal with as free will beings. The power of choice assumes that there is a choice. There is always a choice we can make. The question is, will we do what is necessary to unclench the fist and relax the hand, or do we remain focused on keeping the tension in the hand, so it is tight and shut? Remember back when we were talking about the world of duality.

Lack and abundance are opposing ideas. I do not know anyone who focuses on lack when they want to appreciate and be grateful. They choose to focus on abundance. Culturally, we are conditioned to focus on lack. Like with your clenched fist, you must choose which ideas you will hold onto MORE often, even when you don't realize that you are choosing.

That is free will. Becoming aware of the ideas that no longer serve you, releasing them, and replacing them with something that is more beneficial means you begin to recognize how powerful you are.

3. Thoughts or ideas cause a physical reaction.

The body is the physical vessel in which thoughts and ideas trigger emotions, thus triggering a physical reaction. There is such a thing as a passing thought, one that does not harness our attention in any shape, way, or form. The thoughts that capture our attention are the thoughts that produce physical responses. For simplicity's sake, I categorize physical reactions as either stress-producing or renewal-inducing responses. Stress is not always a harmful thing but it is meant to always be an episode, not an ongoing state. For the sake of our physical health, it is important to note that we are wired to be in a state of renewal—most of the time. The body's stress response is intended for short-lived spurts of necessary energy to keep us out of danger, hyper-focus on important information in a new environment, or get us through an episode of high-intensity emotion. And then the body automatically wants to go back to renewal and well-being. (We can look at any number of examples in the natural world that mimic this process, a zebra being chased, for example.) Notice how contractive feelings are experienced in the body vs expansive feelings. There is a difference. What do you begin to notice when you pay attention?

4. An emotionally induced symptom tends to cause organic change if it persisted long enough.

This results from rule number three being triggered without episodes of renewal that are sufficient for the body to repair and restore. The medical community has long been in agreement that chronic stress wreaks havoc on the body and is a cause for deterioration over time. More importantly, the evidence is growing that a positive attitude, laughter, and the experience of joy and gratitude can have profound effects on people dealing with medical issues, health challenges, and chronic pain and illness. The influence of emotions and the role the mind has on our bodies can no longer be denied.

5. What is expected tends to be realized.

We experience this rule of mind in the generalizations that we carry with us about ourselves in our world. Generalizations typically contain those determining words "always" and "never."

"I never am called upon in class."

"He always ignores me."

"I never get invited anywhere."

Using absolute language like this activates the mind's filters to look for evidence to make that very thing real. Beliefs cloud our expectations; therefore, understanding this rule is important in establishing specific, reasonable, and actionable expectations, knowing that when we put forth expectations, our mind-filters will ultimately look until it finds the evidence to match the belief.

6. Once the subconscious has accepted an idea, it remains until it is replaced by another idea.

The ideas we generate and decide to implement tend to align with what we believe is possible based on our life experiences. Generating ideas is the easy part. Getting that idea to be accepted at a level that the mind can work with is the part that can take some work. Knowing that our belief systems directly filter which ideas can be easily accepted means that we can update and change those beliefs. (Think back to our success equation of awareness, action, time, space, and focus.) This rule is also why hypnosis works so well. Taking those moments to stop and think of a new possibility is not a small, meaningless action. It is the very stepping stone that allows you to move into something new, harnessing the possibility this moment offers to you right now to change your experience!

7. Each suggestion acted upon creates less opposition to each successive suggestion.

Success builds upon success. That is why seemingly small changes in thinking and behavior can have such a tremendous impact on creating lasting, sustainable change. We have to create evidence of our success and celebrate it when we are doing well. One of the most damaging thought patterns we can engage in is the "all or nothing" mentality that demands absolute perfection when establishing new patterns and programs. Anyone who has ever dieted knows this kind of thinking creates a journey of lurking failure around every corner. There is no room for deviation. One donut ends up having the power to throw us off track and erase all the good choices we've been making. Giving in to that suggestion typically reminds us immediately of all the ways that we've been trying to do something and how we continue to fail. Our motivators are simple: avoid pain and/or move towards pleasure. Find the appropriate suggestion within that framework and map out the small ways you can set yourself up for success. Our minds are like puppies; we have to tell it what we want from it consistently, bring it back when it wanders off, and celebrate the small wins, so it understands which suggestions are the beneficial ones to follow.

8. The greater the conscious effort, the less the subconscious response.

This rule exemplifies why "trying" never works. When we try to do something, we are usually coming at it from consciously figuring it out. Trying to fall asleep, trying to lose weight, trying to stop smoking are things I hear from clients every day, and they are all failing at what they want. We are at our best when the conscious and subconscious minds are congruent with one another; each is responsible for different departments of thinking. Our conscious minds can go about mapping out the details of the when, where, and what aspects of actionables that help create our success. The subconscious can concern itself with the how it will all come together, what it feels like to imagine that very thing happening and identifying yet to be seen resources to support us getting there. When we understand how to do this, we harness the power of our minds and become creative solution finders.

I will add my own rule here that I find myself falling into at times and needing to do a reframe.

9. The mind is conditioned to think in the negative.

Clients who arrive in my office always know what they don't want. Rarely are they able to articulate what they do want. When we want to harness the power of the mind, we have to treat it like we are training a puppy. We have to tell it what we want in the affirmative, and we have to be consistent. I know that I struggled with this and needed a lot of practice to get to a place where I can automatically flip things to the affirmative. Here are some examples of flipping negative talk/thoughts to the affirmative. I would also include here no longer accepting any kind of hurtful or deprecating dialogue directed towards yourself.

I don't want to worry anymore. I am capable of trusting.

I can't do anything right. I don't know how to do this yet, but I am learning.

I shouldn't do _____. I can make different choices.

I don't like who I am. I accept myself and know that I am capable of growth.

You always/never do this thing. Right now, I need your help.

These rules can help us begin to dissect our thinking in ways that support creating a new blueprint for our happiness. They offer us a road map to set our internal GPS to a new destination and trust that we can navigate new paths, accepting that detours are sometimes part of the journey.

Looking back at my journey, I can see how these rules were implemented even though it was not done in the methodical way that is laid out here. I can see how realizing my happiness is an inner process instead of an outward contingency plan. I was able to see things that I had not realized until then. Most importantly, I had to stop visualizing myself as a victim of my circumstances. My imagination had played a role in creating the perceived hardships of my life because I believed I needed the hardships in order to "deserve" the good that came my way. I had to step out of my habituated tendency of stress and anger and allow space for a different state of being. Physically, I frequently felt like I was worn out, tired, and stressed because of the emotional states I was consistently residing in. I planned on being stressed out before an activity simply because I thought I needed to be that way so I could be considered important and valued. This program worked for me very successfully for many years. Until it didn't. It wasn't enough to try to be happy. I had to choose to be happy, but choosing happiness didn't suddenly make me happy. I had to build the belief structure that would consistently support that choice. I had to acknowledge my own success, no matter how small the wins seemed. Making the choice was the first step because it provided the necessary GPS my mind needed to know which path to pursue.

Understanding the rules of the mind can help you dissect the things going on in your life right now and help you define steps and actions you can take that will begin to unravel unbeneficial thought patterns and deep-seated programs. Remember the sixth rule, "Once an idea has been accepted by the subconscious, it remains until it is replaced by another idea." Our beliefs color everything we do. Our mind is set to make true in the outer what is played out in the inner world. Start to question those ideas (beliefs) that are holding you back and keeping you stuck. Like a snag on a sweater, you can tug at the yarn and begin to unravel it until it completely loses its shape and its structure. The yarn is still good to make something new, more beneficial, and updated based on new ideas (beliefs) that you choose.

Questions to contemplate:

1. What rule resonates most with you at this point and why? What insight does it provide?

2. How can you utilize this list to unravel old programming and create some fresh ideas that support who you want to be and what you want to do?

3. How does understanding the departments of thinking between conscious and subconscious allow you to map out more effective strategies for creating success?

CHAPTER 8

The Art of Mindlessness and the Power of a Decision

"The next step in human evolution is to transcend thought. This is now our urgent task. It doesn't mean not to think anymore, but simply not to be completely identified with thought, possessed by thought."

This excerpt comes from Eckart Tolle's book *Stillness Speaks*. It is the essence of what I have been talking about throughout this book. Much of our unhappiness comes from the constant narration of our mind, and that narration is filled with judgment, critique, and labeling—all of which keeps us from what is right now. Our thoughts, left to themselves, are typically a falling into the past or jumping forward into the future. Rarely are they grounded in the *now*. Being present does not require the narration of the mind because it is occupied with paying attention to what *is*. When we observe the animal world, we see brilliant examples of presence done with ease, effortless effort. Despite global issues, natural, environmental crises, and other challenges, living creatures are always capable of experiencing renewal and even joyful moments because they are not trying to dissect why things aren't the way they should be. We have that same capacity for renewal and joy, but we have to transcend the mind's narration of never-ending content. This innate capacity is the very thing that allows the kind of happiness, contentment, and appreciation to pour forth without being attached to stuff, attainment, and circumstances.

I have often felt frustration with the process and practice of mindfulness and meditation. It is often expressed because they are "supposed to elevate" presence but when they don't, they can produce feelings of failure because we aren't achieve those states. I have found through my own experience that *trying* to practice mindfulness and/or meditation is the surest way to lead me out of presence. Out for a walk one day with my dog, I became aware that I had been non-thinking the whole time. It was the first time that I became aware of what presence felt like and that I was actually pretty good at it. It had taken me so long to realize this because trying to get it right required the mind's conscious effort to judge what right was. It somehow had to be measured, which cannot be done. It was then I realized it was a sense of mind*less*ness I was after, no longer being aware of the thought-producing mind. And then I realized that I do this fairly often, but I had never given myself credit for it. I now realize that I am a really good meditator. I just do it during my walks instead of cross-legged on the floor. (I am not saying we shouldn't practice meditation and mindfulness but I am inviting you to explore how you can be successful with these practices, without falling into a particular sense or expectation of success.)

If you really explore this idea of mindlessness, most people can recall experiences of it. It naturally happens in those spaces and times when we become the activity we are doing. For some, it happens while they garden, others when they walk or do jigsaw puzzles, others while they are engrossed with a project at work or while sitting quietly on a park bench. We don't give ourselves credit for the restorative value that these episodes offer us. And most of us don't realize the deep sense of contentment these moments provide. Life isn't about being Zen on a mountain top all by yourself (unless you choose it to be). And it certainly isn't about accumulating stuff and running the rat race (unless you choose it to be). Life is about finding that sweet spot of engagement where we can deal with whatever arises in a day with detached responsiveness. This detached responsiveness is the difference between life happening *to* me and me happening *with* life. And there are all kinds of happiness sprinkled throughout being together with life.

Personally, I have found that to have those moments of non-thinking, there is a certain stillness that I need. Stillness is not the absence of sound, but it is the absence of chatter—the buzz feed of noise. The most significant contributor to the chatter in our modern world are the screens that surround us everywhere and even in our pockets. Screens that spew out endless commentary, opinions, and content on anything and everything. And whose only goal is to keep us connected and dialed in for as long as possible. I am not anti-technology, but I am a huge believer that we must be in charge of technology; otherwise, it will be in charge of us. With billions of pieces of information available to us at any given second, I think that we sometimes abdicate the need to think for ourselves. Instead, we weigh in with others to get their opinions and input. Content does not equal wisdom. Wisdom comes from intelligent awareness, a "sense of knowing" that is felt beyond the thinking mind. Without wisdom and awareness, we can find ourselves in a "paralysis by analysis" that leaves us fully incapable of making our own decisions. Your own happiness relies on you to think for yourself, define your own life, and lead it on your terms. How will you ever know your own self without ever being quiet enough to hear the deeper sense of awareness that stillness allows?

Thinking for ourselves and making decisions for what is best for us can be a very scary thing. We want to belong, fit in and be part of our tribes. I have found that every difficult decision I have faced was only difficult because of the fear of judgment I believed I would encounter one way or another. At times, I was almost ready to forgo doing what was right for my family and me to avoid going outside the norm and being judged for it. Looking back, I realize those fears existed only within the chatter of my mind as I was lucky enough to be surrounded by people who ultimately supported me each and every time. It feels good to know that I could be true to myself and my family in those decisions. I am not responsible for anyone beyond myself and my family, so I need to control what the mind chatter is feeding me. I must be willing to be the thinker instead of being the thoughts.

Raising three strong-minded daughters, my husband and I had many opportunities where we had to decide what was best for them as individuals and as a family, even when it meant dancing outside the norm. This included allowing each of them to complete high school in non-traditional ways, like taking time off after high school graduation and pursuing opportunities that are considered outside the norm of higher education. I would not have been able to do these things for them and could not have offered them this level of freedom without questioning my happiness and what drives it. I had to admit that many of the decisions I was making on their behalf were decisions based on what I believed others expected from me. I was compelled to follow the norm for fear of what others would think of me. In exploring these tendencies, I was forced to recognize that we each must pursue our lives according to our internal systems. This is the ultimate "pursuit of happiness," and letting go of the idea that as a mother, I knew what was best for my kids was a belief that I had to relinquish. I am so grateful for the process and experiences that allowed me to recognize this early on in their lives.

The period of time where I knew what was best for them was a short window. I also know that giving up control appropriately over time (which was not easy, to say the least) has left both my husband and me with a tremendous amount of influence now that they are adults. I don't know about you, but being influential over having control seems to be a lot more fun and a lot less effort.

There is a key component in thinking for ourselves that is one of the most powerful conscious actions we can take daily, and that is to make a decision. It is important to fully appreciate this process, especially when we understand the root meaning of this word. In Latin *decidere*, is a combination of two words: de = "off" + *caedere* = "cut." When we think of deciding between cutting off all other options, we provide clarity to the mind. A confused mind tends to choose inaction (paralysis) and is commonly what is giving us the feeling of being stuck. The confusion is created through the mind's ability to create content to fit whatever perception of reality it is filtering. We can talk ourselves into or out of anything. (Parents of teenagers know this well.) The mind needs clarity to know when, where, and how to direct energy, focus, and resources. It needs a clear road map to get clarity. You can't put multiple destinations into a GPS and expect it to go to them at the same time.

We often get stuck in making the "right" decision and, therefore, can stay in that wishy-washy state of confusion out of fear. Here's the thing: the mind ultimately doesn't care; it simply needs a direction. Decisions in and of themselves are not anything but decisions. We make a choice, and something follows. We make another choice; something different ensues. There are consequences to our decisions, and we can decide what serves us best depending on known consequences. There is, however, the rule of unintended consequences, and so there will always be some uncertainty in our decisions. Life is about moving forward in the unknowingness and trusting in our own resilience and the process of life figuring out itself. Our job is to pay attention (or not), to learn (or not), to tweak a process or change course (or not), and to continuously accept life's invitations to learn, grow, explore, investigate and become (or not). We get to decide our level of participation, and that participation sometimes only needs us to make a decision.

In *Think Like a Freak*, the authors, Steven Levitt and Stephen Dubner, construct an experiment where they ask for volunteers to come with a decision that they have wanted to make but haven't figured out the right one yet. They get over 40,000 volunteers who are willing to have the decision made for them via coin toss. There are different life areas and questions but only two choices: heads meant quitting, and tails meant sticking it out. Some of the more popular questions were:

Should I quit my job?

Should I go back to school?

Should I go on a diet?

Should I break a bad habit?

Should I break up with my partner?

The experiment had controls for measuring, follow-up, and accountability, and according to the book, it is still ongoing. Roughly 60% of participants followed the decision of the coin. The data shows that quitting some things tended to produce a higher degree of happiness (quitting a job/ relationship breakup). In comparison, others tended to produce a lesser degree of happiness (asking for a raise, splurging on something fun, signing up for a marathon). Why the level of happiness varied could not be answered, but I find it interesting that people were satisfied enough with the coin toss decision that they were willing to make some significant life changes based on those answers.

To me, this proves that there often are no right answers, just choices. When you come to accept that there is no failure, only feedback, you can see the validity in almost any option. Remember, we can talk ourselves into or out of anything. Make a choice.

This chapter has been about decluttering the mind from the endless flow of content and thinking and making decisions for yourself. I want to end it with reminding you of that acronym I came up with for my clients and who report finding it very beneficial.

S.T.O.P. — **S**pace and **T**ime **O**f **P**ossibility. Simply stop. Stop and breathe. And in that moment of pause, when you exhale out tension and tightness, and you drop into your body, can you begin to contemplate a new possibility for yourself? Can you stop long enough to leave the quagmire of stuff and feel a deeper sense of self? It doesn't take long, just a moment to breathe and drop into your beingness. We have to realize that when we want to make new choices and create new ways of being, we *must* give ourselves space and time to contemplate new possibilities.

Questions to contemplate:

1. How can the idea of mindlessness support you in getting out of the content your mind creates?

2. In what ways can you tweak your thinking to be more intuitive and aligned with your values?

3. If you were to let a coin decide for you right now, what decision would you pose?

CHAPTER 9

The Surest Way to Kill Joy[2]

"Comparing ourselves to others is truly the surest way to kill joy." I saw this on a church marquis when I was feeling particularly down about myself. I felt like it had been put there just for me. Driving past and reading those words, I realized the reason why I was feeling down. I had been comparing myself to a sea of others—the *they* who were doing so much better than me and who were so much more successful, so I thought in my mind. With that awareness, I let go of those impossible-to-meet measurements because there will always be someone more successful than me. I reminded myself that I needed to define my success and measure it against my

---

[2] Original quote is "Comparison is the thief of joy," and has been attributed to President Theodore Roosevelt.

actions and benchmarks. No one else was imposing limitations on me; I was doing it very successfully in my own mind. Again, this is what it means to do internal work and allow external influencing factors to be secondary.

An important aspect of our modern culture that needs to be addressed, if only on a personal level, is the role of social media and how it directly affects our contentment, mental health, and view of the world. Many of us have handed over how we feel about ourselves to algorithms and amounts of likes. There is substantial evidence showing the correlation between declining mental health and the increase in social media usage. Just watching *The Social Dilemma* (Netflix documentary) and listening to former big tech executives talk about prohibiting themselves and their kids from social media are telling about the effects of these platforms. When we mindlessly scroll through endless content and images of what other people are doing, we compare (even if we are not conscious of it) ourselves against curated content that may or may not be real.

We must recognize the choice we have to chase a life of images delivered to us or find our own contentment and joy based on our individual uniqueness, talents, and personality. During the middle school years of raising our daughters, I found myself reminding them that there will always be someone "better "than you and someone who is "worse" than you--always. So why bother going down that rabbit hole? I have to remind myself of this as well--especially as it pertains to my business and what I define as success. I have to check myself after I check social media because frequently, I find myself automatically being pulled into the vortex of comparisons. This is where mindfulness (awareness) is extremely beneficial. It's not about NEVER comparing yourself but what we do with it and how we respond to it. And it is a totally different animal when we are making choices of how far down the rabbit hole we go and how long we want to stay there. Coming back into ourselves is our CHOICE, and it is easier to do if we are not in a constant stream of idyllic visuals that have been filtered for optical pleasure.

I am always surprised to hear how many young adults say that they don't like social media and how it makes them feel, yet they feel powerless to disconnect from it. When I work with clients on personal contentment (no matter their age), we always discuss social media. Many times, I challenge them to do a social media cleanse to give them a chance to see the effects and to notice whatever differences they observe in the absence of social media. After recognizing his own gluttonous appetite for likes, shares, and comments that validated his ego and his experiences, one client decided to do a full-on purge. His original commitment was for thirty days. These thirty days were not without struggle. He had to look for ways to validate himself, find different ways to communicate with those he chose to communicate with, deal with his boredom when it flared, get comfortable with his own thoughts about what he was doing, and trust that he was okay without relying on feedback from others, and reinvent who he was in the dating pool as there was no "social proof" he could fall back on.

We know that the learning is in the struggle, so the discoveries made within those thirty days of reflection were plenty. He discovered:

- a realization of how much his and others' online presence is all about creating carefully constructed illusions;
- how much more time and attention he now had to allocate to his passion projects, business endeavors, and relationships in physical reality;

- a shift from reliance on, and longing for, external validation of others to an extreme amount of internal validation and self-confidence;
- a sense of freedom from now only engaging in activities that he was intrinsically compelled to do, rather than doing things he perceived others would most approve of (doing activities just to get a photo to build his personal brand and get more likes);
- a release from societal expectations which allowed him to live more in tune with his internal compass;
- an abundance of awareness and the ability to be fully immersed in the present moment, without social media constantly nagging at his attention in the background of his mind;
- the ability to live every moment in the present and no longer needed to debate whether or not to document the moment with a photo;
- the shift to a more egoless existence because it was no longer fed artificial content;
- a more vivid lens on how reality actually is since he is no longer being inundated by propaganda and advertisements on a daily basis;

- his spending addiction subsided due to no longer being exposed to pinpointed advertisements on a daily basis;
- he now brought more awareness, attention, and energy to real-life social interactions since social obligations were no longer nagging at his attention from the apps on the phone in his pocket;
- it motivated him into even more self-improvement and to put his best foot forward in social interactions since he no longer had a digital resume of his "awesomeness" to speak for him or to fall back on;
- an awareness of the inflation of some people's egos due to their social media presence thinking they can get away with acting like monsters in real life, and to those in their immediate surroundings; and
- he no longer had a measuring stick to compare his life to others on a daily basis, so now he lives his life's journey at his own pace, with no need to rush to complete *The List* like the majority of his friends whose photo ops use to fill his newsfeeds and mind on a daily basis.

These awarenesses came because of his willingness to embark on a really difficult journey, but he was willing to stick with it to realize his growth. This client has gone on to extend his purge to a full-on deletion of most of his social media accounts. This may not be everyone's choice because social media does absolutely have benefits, many of which we have seen during the Covid pandemic. They offer us powerful platforms where we can feel more connected, and this is good. What is clearly illustrated is the need to be the master and not the servant of our technology. Giving yourself the time to observe how you are with and without social media can be a very beneficial process to go through so you are ultimately in control of its influence and have a solid awareness of when you are about to drop into the rabbit hole.

The take-away here is to understand the power of these platforms and technology in general. Remember, you want to be the master of these platforms and not their servant. You have to know that when you engage in social media, *you* are the product, and the algorithms are devised to feed you precisely the information that is appealing to you based on your engagement. Engagement equals information; the more you engage, the more specific information advertisers have to market very directly to you. They are paying money to keep you engaged as long as possible with the intent of getting you to click through to an offer of some kind. The longer you stay engaged, the greater the chance you click through. Take control of your online presence and engage deliberately, consciously, and in limited amounts of time. And if you are a parent, please understand how vulnerable and susceptible children are to the manipulative persuasions of these powerful platforms.

Questions to contemplate:

1. In what ways is social media beneficial to your well-being?

2. In what ways is social media detrimental to your well-being?

3. How can you empower yourself to more beneficially manage your use of social media?

CHAPTER 10

The Process of Growth

The realization of my own unhappiness has been the catalyst for me to pursue a deeper understanding of myself. Without my *unhappiness*, I would never have embarked on a journey of discovering what I am capable of. The very struggle of unhappiness ultimately led to a broader, deeper, more expanded version, a truer version of satisfaction and contentment. This journey followed a process of order, disorder, and re-order—a natural progression that allows for the transformation of self and our own identity in the world.

Richard Rohr talks about this process in his book *The Universal Christ*. Reading his words, I was able to identify that this was the process I was going through all those years ago, though I was not capable of knowing it to be a beneficial process at the time. Hindsight is 20/20. There are three phases to the process.

The first phase, *order*, is the belief that we are safe, comfortable, and innocent. Not all people are afforded this phase of order, but those who are often have a feeling of *rightness* about what they have achieved, almost to the degree of smugness. This was me checking off all of the boxes of happiness; for a time, there was a rightness about achieving that list. Rohr sites that in this phase, people often feel the necessity to protect what is theirs because it is a worldview based on lack, control, and fear. It is the comfort zone where deep questioning is rarely happening. I one hundred percent agree with his definition and know that this was my worldview way back when.

Disorder, the second phase, is the breaking down of the established norms (or the perceived established norms) from the first phase. Realizing my unhappiness was the beginning of my disorder. Mine was an internal disorder, as my external circumstances did not change. Disorder can happen internally, outwardly, or both. Often it is circumstantial disorder (crisis) that leads to internal disorder: the death of a loved one, a health challenge, etc. Disorder can be chaotic, which can cause us to forget the necessity for it. The comfort zone has to be broken up for any learning to occur. If we want a new kitchen, we have to demolish and take out the old one first. Space must be created for something new to come in. Most of us do not willingly enter into the disorder. Chaos and crisis usually thrust their way upon us, where we are forced to respond and think differently. I don't remember precisely what caused me to realize my lack of happiness. Some awareness offered itself in a flash of insight. That awareness was the beginning of my disorder process. This disorder can happen in macro and micro experiences which adds to the learning process.

As of this writing, we are in a period of greatly needed macro disorder. Exposure of what is no longer working is happening all around us. Covid has been the catalyst for some of this exposure as well as the many social injustices and political discord not to mention environmental crises. Knowing that this disorder is a necessary part of the process allows me to trust that: solutions will be found, there is an unseen order to the chaos, and space is being made for new ideas and processes that will be more inclusive, supportive, and sustainable. My job is to pay attention to my role within my space and within my tribe and do what I am called to do to move through whatever micro disorder is being presented to me. We can't always affect change on a large scale but we can affect it in the detail of our own experience.

This brings us to the last phase: *reorder*. Reorder is the new order established after the disorder, and it is based on the learning and wisdom gained from the chaos and/or pain. It is the light at the end of the tunnel. Reorder is never a going back to "what was" but is a promise of realizing a new possibility, a deeper understanding, and a higher realization of who we can be, what we can do, and where we can go. It is the creative process that aligns with cooperation, collaboration, and inclusivity. Reorder is grounded in abundance, surrender, and love.

I now know that this process is ongoing and is a natural process of life. I can more easily embrace the periods of struggle. This knowledge has also allowed me to be more comfortable as a mother observing my children's struggles. I cannot move through the process for them; I can only trust that they are resilient enough to move through it themselves, just as I must trust that I can move through whatever is my struggle. This doesn't mean that I don't worry and just skip through life without a care. It means that I feel more capable of determining how long I want to stay in states of worry, confusion, and anxiety. I feel empowered to move into a more beneficial way of being.

Whether we have a spiritual practice or not, we can use this process of order, disorder, and reorder to guide us through a deeper understanding of ourselves. Spirituality isn't required, but it can be helpful. If you feel like something is missing, perhaps exploring your own spirituality is something that brings benefit to you. Being without any spiritual connection was something I felt I was lacking and wanted to explore. This ongoing exploration has helped ground me in a more expanded vision of what life is. I have come to believe that there are many different ways to connect to the largeness of the unknowable some of us refer to as God, and there are and have been many enlightened teachers that have shown us ways to our divine unfoldment.

According to my spiritual teachings, Advent (the four weeks before Christmas) is the awaiting of the Christ child. I appreciate how my spiritual home (Unity) has made the story of the birth of Jesus a promise for each of us to recognize our own Christ self; it is not limited to only one person. Divinity is extended to each and every one of us, and the coming of Christ is the coming of the divine in each person. It is a realization that the divinity in Jesus is in all of us, and we can use this journey to awaken to that Divine within (or not). This Divinity may be referred to as life force, soul, energy, spirit, or any other name you choose, for it cannot ever be fully defined; it transcends race, religion, gender, and all other "separating factors"—it is a unifying principle that we are, at our very core, all the same. The time of Advent is used to reflect upon and deepen our understanding of the aspects of this energy that we are. During Advent, we are invited to focus on the attributes of hope and faith, peace, joy, and love. We discuss how these things are within us all the time, that they are abundant in nature and ever-present—constant truths about our very core. But we are required to connect to them, activate them, and remember that they are there for us--not only to be discussed but also to be experienced. In remembering, we birth our true nature, and this process is not limited to once a year, on a particular day. We can birth our Divinity and let it come forward any moment of any day.

Exploring my need for a deeper connection to unifying principles allowed me to experience how this has led me to greater acceptance of so much of life. That greater acceptance has directly impacted the degree of happiness I experience because it has also greatly expanded my understanding of meaningful happiness. Knowing that the birth of Christ is not limited to one individual and the birth of the Divine is not an event, but a process led me to contemplate the metaphor of the birthing process itself. Birth never happens without first experiencing contractions. Contractions being the necessary mechanism by which expansion happens. Birth only happens with contractions. Upon further exploration, we see this pattern in nature as well: a fragile stem bursting through the hull of a seed, baby chicks having to peck their way through a protective shell, a butterfly struggling to break free of a cocoon that has become confining. All of these are examples of the necessity of contractions before expansion. This leads me to believe that the same is necessary for emotional, mental, and spiritual growth. That the struggle we all try our best to avoid is the exact thing that propels us to the next level, and yet we work so hard at fighting these struggles, judging ourselves as unworthy, not enough, valueless because we feel we don't fit the cookie-cutter definition of success. It is the struggle (contraction) for which we create the depth of our experience in this life, and we need to allow ourselves to move through it, break through it, and accept it as a natural part of the journey. Along the way, we realize the Divine qualities within—strength, creativity, acceptance, love, release, and so many more. Our challenges are not punishments, and we certainly haven't done anything to *deserve* them. They are the life journey of being human in all its unique facets; they are the opportunity for us to burst forth, learn, and rise to the next level. It is the journey itself of defining happiness in the small moments of awakening to what we are capable of, how we show up, how we serve in relation to others, and to discover our purpose. Happiness is not something that can be looked for. Happiness is something that must be found. It is right there for you, in its entirety in the small moments of now. Will you see them?

You may be on a journey where you too feel this elusive sense of missing something, of not being *enough* just like I did and, on some days, still do. Know that these are not reflections of deficiency in you but an invitation to explore and go beyond what you know to be true right now. Whether that invitation leads you to spiritual discovery, to a new business venture, or embarking on a long-desired trip, it doesn't matter. Life's invitations happen in so many ways. The important thing is to remember to create the time and space where you are allowing yourself to do what is in alignment with your values, desires, and beliefs. There is no limit to our good and the good that we can contribute back in meaningful ways. Question limiting beliefs, welcome periods of disorder, seek inner wisdom and trust that it is there, get more comfortable with silence, know that you are enough. Be willing to make it up as you go along because we are all doing it anyway. The only road to happiness is the one that allows you to discover all that you are here to be. It is the road that accepts the potholes, the detours, the wrong turns, the scenic view, the construction zones, and the rest stops. It is an invitation to forget what you think you know about happiness and embark on the journey of defining and discovering it for yourself.

Questions to contemplate:

1. Looking back, what challenges have you gone through that led you to a "breakthrough?"

2. What happens when you embrace a current challenge and lean into knowing it is exactly what is needed to get you to the next part of the journey?

3. How can you surrender to "what is" so you can more creatively move through it?

CHAPTER 11

Happiness Is Now

One of the reasons I decided to write this book is to offer my struggle with finding happiness because I have so many clients experiencing similar revelations. Many of us have been conditioned to believe in an outward path to happiness, and it fails, maybe not right away, but at some point, it fails. My own inner journey, work with clients and my role as a wife and mother shows me time and time again that we all have our own best answers if we will just trust ourselves to explore them. To explore them, we have to create a mindset that allows them to come forth in whatever way they come forth. I have found that allowing, surrendering, and accepting are processes that make it easier for creative resources and states of mind to flow. These concepts can seem counterintuitive in a culture where we readily accept the idea that we are always in competition, where scarcity and lack are assumed, and where we are taught validation and worth come from our external environment. Tremendous power is unleashed when we surrender. I hope that this book has offered some insight for you to create your reality based on more beneficial practices and gentler ways of being. If you would like more information or want to have a conversation about my services, please feel free to reach out to me through the contact information at the end of this book.

Following are the concepts and practices that are a way to experience more peace, joy, and contentment. They are by no means an exhaustive list. Coupled with whatever you choose to pursue and attain, these practices remind us that there is something more than just acquiring, and they help us to remain grounded. You might recognize many of these as things you've heard before. That is the beautiful thing about realizing blanket statements of truth, we always come back to the same things, and we always come back to ourselves.

My experience with practicing with what is listed (to the best of my ability on any given day) has led to greater ease with life. This ease does not mean that my life is free from challenges, but it does mean that I can be less rigid and more open without the need to force things to happen in a particular way on a particular timeline. Ease is unforced effort, not the absence of effort. My hope for you is to be more at ease in your own life, and I trust that you find your way to more enjoyment, calm, and contentment by discovering your own definition of happiness. (The list is in no particular order).

1. Breathe
2. Become comfortable with and in silence.
3. Be in nature.
4. Practice surrendering and trusting.
5. Notice your language patterns.
6. Move your body.
7. Go screenless.
8. Ask high-quality questions.
9. Notice intellectual overdrive.
10. Embrace the moment of now.

1. Breathe! We all hear this over and over— "Just breathe." The power of this cannot be overestimated because it is the fastest way to affect change in the body. Change what the body is doing, and we change what the mind does. We easily access the vagus nerve through slow,

deep breathing. It's like sending a text message to the mind/body that says, "It's safe for me to relax." It is impossible to move out of an anxious-filled state without changing our breath. And because we are free will beings, we can decide to do this proactively.

2. Become comfortable with and in silence. Our modern world is filled with chatter. Outer chatter can affect inner chatter. Being comfortable with silence allows us an opportunity to drop into our bodies and quiet the mind as well. This can take time and practice if we are not used to it. At the end of most yoga practices, the final resting pose of savasana is practiced. Savasana means "corpse pose." It is a pose of relaxation and quiet. I often fought against this last pose because I believed it unnecessary and a waste of time until I heard an instructor explain its purpose. We do savasana to give the body time to absorb all the information it processed during the full practice. Because we give it this time, the body more deeply takes in the benefits of the exercise. It is a time of absorption. I love this definition. Silence is time for the mind to process, absorb and also release. Be willing to be silent, and you might be surprised by what you end up hearing.

3. Be in nature. The positive effects of nature on our psyche can usually be felt instantaneously. Noticing trees, lakes, beaches, mountains, sun, clouds, rain, snow, and animals reminds us that we are only one aspect of life. Nature can bring us back into simplicity. Watching a dog chase its tail reminds us of our playful nature and capacity for joy. Just watching a cat lounge in the sun can permit us to do the same, if only for a moment. Nature always just IS. It is a powerful reminder of this moment.

4. Practice surrendering and trusting. Anytime we experience worry/anxiety, a need for control, and rigid thinking, it usually is a good indicator that we are not trusting, and we are shut off from creative problem-solving. Surrender doesn't mean giving up. It is an opportunity to relax the body and accept that we might not have all of the information about a particular issue. Trusting assumes that we will receive whatever information and/or resource is necessary to move through whatever challenge we face, and until then, we can go on with something else. You may have heard the phrase, "It's all good." I like the continuation of that, "It's all good. And if it ain't good yet, it ain't over." Trusting allows us to move through our day

without continuing to think about whatever we are dealing with.

5. Notice your language patterns. Most of us, through conditioning, tend to use negative language. Be willing to practice and flip to the affirmative. Remember that our words and thoughts have energetic frequencies. We have tremendous power in putting out "good vibes" through just our everyday language. You'll be amazed at how this practice can transform how you feel in your day-to-day experience. This is one of the most direct ways we can "be the change we wish to see." Please note, I am not talking about positive thinking and pretending like everything is rainbows and butterflies. I am laying out a way to see challenges and frame them to empower us to move through them in the most beneficial way possible. Committing to being kind to yourself in your inner dialogue is an important change that you can make right now. We say things to ourselves that we would never say to a complete stranger. Clean up your inner dialogue and verbal language and reap the immediate benefits.

6. Move your body. Movement, along with laughter, is the best medicine. Find ways to give your body (your vehicle) what it needs in some way that feels good to you every day. It doesn't

have to be a full-on workout. The best way to create an ongoing practice is to find something that feels good to *you*! Stop excusing yourself from movement and just do it. The effects of movement in relieving the mind of anxiety, worry, and stress are undeniable. Consistent physical movement and activity also act as a savings account. Your body becomes stronger, more flexible, with a more robust immune system, so if something does happen (injury, sickness, illness), you tend to recover more quickly with less downtime.

7. Go screenless. Take time every day to turn off *all* screens. Our devices are powerful tools with tremendous capabilities. We must, however, be the master of the tool and not the servant. Making time to disconnect consciously has benefits, but it can feel unfamiliar if we are not used to doing it. Experts are identifying "phone addiction" as a real thing, and people report that they feel like part of them is missing without their phone. To be the master, we have to be okay without the device. We must know how to limit screen time and do other things. Our devices are the biggest obstacle to more meaningful engagement with others and our day-to-day experience. Be okay to be without them.

8. Ask high quality questions. The quality of our questions determines the quality of our answers. *If* questions give you conditional answers. *How* questions assume a successful outcome. *Why* questions take you to the past. *What, when, where,* and *how* move you forward.

9. Notcie intellectual overdrive. Intellectual overdrive can also be described as paralysis by analysis. It's when you are spinning in your head and no longer have access to creative problem-solving. (You do not have access to a creative, imaginative mind when the conscious mind is in overdrive. Use the acronym S.T.O.P. — Space, Time Of Possibility.) Know that the intellectual mind is only one aspect of you, and you need not have so much power. Drop into your body. Breathe. Feel your body. Breathe. Remind yourself of your resilience and ability to respond to them right now. Allow intuition to rise up and support you.

10. Embrace the moment of now. Life unfolds in the now. This moment is all you and I have. The entirety of the natural world reflects this. Existence is only ever happening right now. When we remember that our life is one continuous moment of now, we can more easily release the past (taking acquired wisdom with us) and let go of the need to control a future that

has not yet happened. In doing this, we realize our ability to respond to whatever needs responding to right now. We can only ever have a thought, feel a feeling, or take action at the moment. The past no longer is. The future is not here, so boldly BE right now.

For more information or to connect with Kelli, please visit:

www.kellivon.com

www.westmetrohypnosis.com

https://www.facebook.com/kellihypnotist/

Speaking engagement inquiries can be made to Kelli@kellivon.com

Made in the USA
Coppell, TX
04 August 2022